TABLE OF CONTENTS

Introduction – This is How I Explain It

Chapter 1 - This is How WikiHow Explains It:

Chapter 2 – This is How Traders.com Explains It

Chapter 3 – This is How Wisdom Financial Explains It

Chapter 4 – This is How CoolTrade Explains It

Chapter 5 – This is How Binary Options Explains It

Chapter 6 – This is How Randolph Read Explains It

Chapter 7 – This is How InvestorGuide.com Explains It

Chapter 8 – This is How The Minimalist Guide Explains It

I Have a Special Gift for My Readers

Meet the Author

How to Choose a Good Trading System
Get it Right the First Time to Maximize Trading Profits
©Copyright 2013 by Dr. Leland Benton

DISCLAIMER AND TERMS OF USE AGREEMENT:

(Please Read This Before Using This Book)

This information is for educational and informational purposes only. The content is not intended to be a substitute for any professional advice, diagnosis, or treatment.

The author and publisher of this book and the accompanying materials have used their best efforts in preparing this book.

The author and publisher make no representation or warranties with respect to the accuracy, applicability, fitness, or completeness of the contents of this book. The information contained in this book is strictly for educational purposes. Therefore, if you wish to apply ideas contained in this book, you are taking full responsibility for your actions.

The author and publisher disclaim any warranties (express or implied), merchantability, or fitness for any particular purpose.

The author and publisher shall in no event be held liable to any party for any direct, indirect, punitive, special, incidental or other consequential damages arising directly or indirectly from any use of this material, which is provided "as is", and without warranties. As always, the advice of a competent legal, tax, accounting, medical or other professional should be sought where applicable.

The author and publisher do not warrant the performance, effectiveness or applicability of any sites listed or linked to in this book. All links are for information purposes only and are not warranted for content, accuracy or any other implied or explicit purpose.

This book is © Copyrighted by ePubWealth.com. No part of this may be copied, or changed in any format, or used in any way other than what is outlined within this course under any circumstances. Violators will be prosecuted.

Introduction – This is How I Explain It

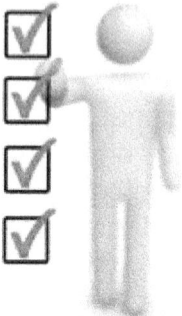

Choosing a Trading System That Actually Works

In writing this book, my GOAL (remember this word please) is to make you aware of various viewpoints on selecting a trading system that fits your needs.

It is important that your NEEDS be defined by your GOALS!! Your goal should be to make money – YES; however in my book "**Money Is an Effect and Not a Cause** http://www.amazon.com/dp/B008ZGM2MK, I define money as the result of smart investing. In other words, money should never be thought of as a "cause" but as an "effect"! Money is simply a commodity that you buy and sell!

As you read the various viewpoints, you will begin to see a pattern emerge; a pattern of similar recommendations to consider, your goals notwithstanding. When approaching the market, always be cautious and conservative until you are comfortable and knowledgeable in what you are trading.

I believe a good trading system should be considered for inclusion in one's portfolio in order to potentially enjoy superior returns. Finding a good trading system, however, can be a very difficult process. So it becomes necessary to have a way of distinguishing good systems from the rest. Fortunately, there is a way to do this by using a demanding set of criteria that I believe must be met in order for you to consider using the system.

The purpose of this book is to define the criteria that I believe will enable you to identify the good systems out there from all the rest.

Criteria

Listed below are the key elements of the criteria set you should use in evaluating a trading system. A good trading system will meet the requirements of each key element whereas many systems will only meet some requirements. For example, a trading system may be advertised as having 80% winning trades which sounds pretty good. However, that same system's losing trades may be 5 times higher than the average winning trade, making the system a net loser.

Mechanical System

The trading system must be 100% mechanical without any human input or overrides. It must also not be tweaked or adjusted as time goes on to fit current data. Also, the system algorithms or rules must not be curve-fitting or tailored to short term, non-repetitive patterns of past data that eliminate otherwise losing trades. A good way to screen for curve-fitting is to look for consistently good results over a minimum of 5 years of past data that meet all of the other criteria outlined in this report as well.

Liquid Markets

The trading system should be aimed at liquid markets where sufficient daily volume exists to easily and consistently execute orders as intended by the system with a minimum of slippage. For example, the S&P 500 Index Futures Market is highly liquid, whereas the Orange Juice Futures Market is far less liquid.

Market Direction Independence

A good trading system will not be dependent on a bull market for its success. It should have the potential to generate successful trading performance in all market conditions; bull, bear, and sideways trading range.

Hypothetical Performance Results

The primary way of evaluating a trading system is based on its historical back tested performance ("hypothetical performance"). But the performance record must include real world trading commission and slippage assumptions.

Commission and slippage can cause an otherwise winning performance to actually be a net loser. Beware of any futures trading system performance data where commission and slippage assumptions are not included or are understated.

The trading system must be 100% mechanical without any human input or overrides.

Maximum Drawdown

An inherent characteristic of investing in general and in trading systems in particular is the maximum drawdown in account value from the most recent peak. This is a very important factor in assessing the risk associated with any system. There are two aspects to consider; the dollar amount of the drawdown as a percentage of the total account value (should not exceed ½ of the average annual return) and the duration of the drawdown until a new peak level in equity is realized (should not exceed 6 months).

Some trading systems hype great profits over the past several years, but don't disclose drawdowns that sometimes exceed the initial capital invested and last for a year or more. Before selecting a trading system, you must be able to quantify the drawdown risk and find it suitable, both financially and emotionally.

Beginning Account Size

The maximum past drawdown (over a minimum five year period) plus the margin required for one contract is the absolute minimum account size required to trade a system. And to be conservative, it is prudent to add a buffer since the maximum drawdown for any trading system is always in the future.

Annual Returns

Annual returns are measured as net profit after commissions and slippage, divided by the beginning account size which gives you annual percent return on beginning account size.

Two things are important here. First, the average annual net profit should be a minimum of twice the maximum drawdown over a period of at least 5 years. Second, ideally there should be no losing years.*

Before selecting a trading system, you must be able to quantify the drawdown risk and find it suitable, both financially and emotionally.

Trade Profile

There are two aspects important here. First, the percent of profitable trades should be in the 40-60% range and the ratio of average win to average loss should be in the 1.3 - 2.0 range. Second, the average trade net profit (total net profits divided by the total number of all trades) should be at a minimum 3 times greater than real world per trade slippage and commission assumptions.

Beware of systems claiming to deliver greater than 60% winners. Such systems usually exhibit a very poor average win to average loss ratio where a few losing trades can easily wipe out profits from several winning trades.

You Now Have the Tools

By following the guidelines in this report, I believe you are now in a position to distinguish the difference between good systems that have the potential to deliver superior returns and the rest. Remember, a trading system must meet all of the criteria elements outlined here to qualify as a system that you would consider trading for your own account.

The Next Move Is Yours

Trading systems are not for everyone. In particular, futures trading involves significant risk and should only be considered by those who have determined that futures trading is appropriate for them with regard to their financial situation. However, the appropriate use of a good automated trading system could mean the difference between mediocre and superior returns. I believe you now have the tools necessary to properly evaluate a trading system. I hope this report has been informative and adds to your success in the future.

Remember, a trading system must meet all of the criteria elements outlined here to qualify as a system that you would consider trading for your own account.

*Futures trading is not appropriate for everyone. There is a substantial risk of loss associated with trading futures. Losses can and will occur. No system or methodology has ever been developed that can guarantee profits or ensure freedom from losses. No representation or implication is being made that using the Instant Profits methodology or system will generate profits or ensure freedom from losses.

Chapter 1 - This is How WikiHow Explains It:

http://www.wikihow.com/Choose-a-Trading-System-That-Actually-Works

☐ 1 **Mechanical System**: The trading system must be 100% mechanical without any human input or overrides. It must also not be tweaked or adjusted as time goes on to fit current data. Also, the system algorithms or rules must not be curve-fitting or tailored to short term, non-repetitive patterns of past data that eliminate otherwise losing trades. A good way to screen for curve-fitting is to look for consistently good results over a minimum of 5 years of past data that meet all of the other criteria outlined in this report as well.

☐ 2 **Liquid Markets**: The trading system should be aimed at liquid markets where sufficient daily volume exists to easily and consistently execute orders as intended by the system with a minimum of slippage. For example, the S&P 500 Index Futures

Market is highly liquid, whereas the Orange Juice Futures Market is far less liquid.

☐ 3 **Market Direction Independence**: A good trading system will not be dependent on a bull market for its success. It should have the potential to generate successful trading performance in all market conditions; bull, bear, and sideways trading range.

☐ 4 **Hypothetical Performance Results**: The primary way of evaluating a trading system is based on its historical back tested performance hypothetical performance. But the performance record must include real world trading commission and slippage assumptions. Commission and slippage can cause an otherwise winning performance to actually be a net loser. Beware of any futures trading system performance data where commission and slippage assumptions are not included or are understated.

☐ 5 **Maximum Drawdown**: An inherent characteristic of investing in general and in trading systems in particular is the maximum drawdown in account value from the most recent peak. This is a very important factor in assessing the risk associated with any system. There are two aspects to consider; the dollar amount of the drawdown as a percentage of the total account value (should not exceed of the average annual return) and the duration of the drawdown until a new peak level in equity is realized (should not exceed 6 months).

Some trading systems hype great profits over the past several years, but dont disclose drawdowns that sometimes exceed the initial capital invested and last for a year or more. Before selecting a trading system, you must be able to quantify the drawdown risk and find it suitable, both financially and emotionally.

☐ 6 **Beginning Account Size**: The maximum past drawdown (over a minimum five year period) plus the margin required for one contract is the absolute minimum account size required to trade a system. And to be conservative, it is prudent to add a buffer since the maximum drawdown for any trading system is always in the future.

☐ 7 **Annual Returns**: Annual returns are measured as net profit after commissions and slippage, divided by the beginning account size which gives you annual percent return on beginning account size. Two things are important here. First, the average annual net profit should be a minimum of twice the maximum drawdown over a period of at least 5 years. Second, ideally there should be no losing years.

☐ 8 **Trade Profile**: There are two aspects important here. First, the percent of profitable trades should be in the 40-60% range and the ratio of average win to average loss should be in the 1.3 - 2.0 range. Second, the average trade net profit (total net profits divided by the total number of all trades) should be at a minimum 3 times greater than real world per trade slippage and commission assumptions. Beware of systems claiming to deliver greater than 60% winners. Such systems usually exhibit a very poor average win to average loss ratio where a few losing trades can easily wipe out profits from several winning trades.

☐ 9 **If you want to learn more about developing the Forex strategy that is right for you, consider your options carefully**. Studies have shown that people learn more effectively when they watch demonstrations of live trading. Also, when you have the ability to use a demo account to make practice traders you can test your new strategy and work with your Forex trading system to ensure that it is configured the way that you need it to work.

Chapter 2 – This is How Traders.com Explains It
Written by Carley Garner

http://www.traders.com/index.php/sac-magazine/current-contents/q-a-a/futures-for-you/1844-choosing-a-trading-platform

What criteria should I use for choosing a trading platform?

It is in the best interests of brokerage firms to make it as easy as possible for their clients to trade. After all, they generate revenue on each transaction and the more convenient it is to enter an order, the more commission they could earn.

Accordingly, brokerage firms have worked hard to provide each type of trader an attractive trading solution.

Unfortunately, finding the appropriate platform for your circumstances can be a cumbersome task. Platforms come in all sizes, costs, and specialties, but not all brokerage firms offer all platforms. Further, even platforms developed by third-party vendors likely have different data providers and will certainly have differing margin rules across various brokerage firms. This is because the brokers and exchanges set margin policy, not the platform. Thus, traders should consider their choice of brokerage house and platform within the same process.

Several futures trading platforms are offered to clients for free. In fact, most brokerage firms will offer at least one no-cost order entry solution. In the past, free platforms were challenged in features, but now, there are some highly capable complimentary offerings. Many include real-time and streaming quotes on options and futures, and perhaps even a nice charting package.

For the casual position trader, these often meet their needs and make premium (and costly) platforms unnecessary. Nonetheless, daytraders or swing traders who need a more robust application might find it worthwhile to pay a little more for increased functionality. In the end, the goal is to make money, not to save it. If having premium charts and order entry will help your strategy, then it is money well spent.

Paid platforms provide traders with access to streaming real-time quotes with deluxe charting and point & click order entry capabilities, but bear in mind it might be necessary to purchase price data in addition to the trading software. Although many of the free platforms provide similar functions, paid-for platforms advertise low-latency execution, more convenient order entry features, more user-friendly charting, the ability to automate strategies, and may even allow you to develop your own indicators.

For instance, these types of platforms enable traders to enter multiple entry prices when trading more than one contract. Once filled, they can instruct the platform to place multiple exit orders at various prices and even trail stop-loss orders higher to protect open profits. Traders might also program the platform to enter a trade if particular events occur, such as specific prices being hit or oscillators behaving in a certain way.

These types of orders are known as *contingency* orders because they depend on a specific event occurring. Traders should be aware of whether such orders are held "server-side" or on the trader's computer. Contingent orders rely on software to execute or cancel them based on another event occurring. If you utilize them, it is a good idea to choose a platform capable of holding the accompanying execution instructions on an offsite server and not your computer. This is because in a server-side arrangement, your orders will still be working and executed even if your personal computer loses connection, or crashes.

Some platforms charge a monthly fee, but many upgraded ones charge a usage fee on a per-side basis. This means that a set fee is charged to the trading account each time a trade is executed. I have witnessed fees ranging from as high as $1.50 per side to as low as $0.15. The brokerage firm often subsidizes platform costs that fall on the lower end.

Remember: a trade consists of two sides, referred to as a *round turn*. A trader being charged a per-side platform fee would be charged when entering the market and again when exiting.

I have found the functionality difference between platforms charging a fee on the high end of the price range relative to the low end is minimal. The higher-priced platforms tend to offer automated system trading and development to justify higher fees while others charge higher transaction fees, claiming to offer faster server communication. For those not developing and implementing proprietary systems or scalping small intraday price moves, less costly platforms are often recommended.

Traders who intend to do a considerable amount of volume may be better off choosing a platform that offers flat monthly fees as opposed to transaction-based fees. But lower-volume traders know they pay only for what they use. While $0.15 per side doesn't seem like a lot, it is equal to $0.30 per round turn and $300 for those trading 1,000 round turns a month. There are flat monthly subscription-based platforms in this price range, but most go for far less with chart capabilities and order entry features to meet the needs of most traders.

Choosing the right platform for your situation is challenging, but choosing the wrong platform can be an expensive mistake. Consult with a good broker for guidance!

Chapter 3 – This is How Wisdom Financial Explains It

http://www.wisdomfinancialinc.com/resources/learn-about-trading/trading-systems-explained/

Trading Systems: What you need to know before investing.

<u>What exactly is a Futures Trading System?</u> Futures trading systems are an automatic, computerized method of placing buy and sell orders. Trading systems software utilize the latest advanced computer technology to provide mathematical models based on past market prices, trends, divergence, momentum and other indicators.

<u>Why use a Futures Trading System?</u> Emotional decision making is often a trader's worst enemy (greed, fear, disbelief, etc.) System trading removes this emotional element from trading. In fact, many top-performing Commodity Trading Advisors now rely heavily upon computerized trading system software.

Besides eliminating second-guessing, whims and uninformed decision making, the advantages of using a disciplined, systematic approach to trading are numerous:

- A trading system generates instructions based solely on predetermined rules.
- A trading system can be tested and researched prior to committing actual capital to trade.
- A trading system can specify correct capitalization levels based on simulated performance, risk and draw-downs.
- The system rules determine the timing for order placement, not the trader.
- The trading system is emotionless; the system does not believe, feel, worry or obsess over a trade.
- System speculation is objective, disciplined, quantitative, technical, logical and precise.

Bottom line: Trading systems provide the much needed structure to trading. Each order placed is governed by a predetermined set of rules that does not deviate based on anything other than market action. A trading system will include specific money management parameters and the mechanical placement of those orders insures those rules are being followed.

The questions you should be asking right now...

1) <u>Is a Trading System right for me?</u> A cardinal rule of successful trading: Adopt a definite trading plan. Because of the emotional stress inherent in any speculative situation, you must have a predetermined method of operation. That includes a

set of rules you must adhere to in order to protect yourself from making irrational decisions.

Software for futures trading offers you the disciplined and unemotional approach to trading that can potentially increase your odds. In addition, the sheer processing power of a computerized trading system ensures that a watchful eye is kept on the markets around the clock. It would be impossible for a human trader to constantly monitor and analyze all global markets 24 hours a day.

To further highlight the value of following a system, here is a brief comparison of common characteristics of discretionary versus systems trading:

Discretionary Trader	System Trader
Rarely trades with a plan	Has a predetermined pla
Generally follows the "hot" market	Participates in many ma sectors
Spends hours analyzing markets	Spends minutes prepari the next day
Overexposed in a single market	Diversified into multip sectors
Generally undercapitalized	Properly capitalized portfolio performance
Erratic trading results	Accepts his/her share c losses

2) <u>Which Trading System should I use?</u> There are as many trading systems to choose from as there

are trading objectives – plus new systems being developed as quickly as market dynamics change. So, in order to answer that question, you're going to have to do a bit of exploring.

Considerations include:

Knowledge – System trading requires a basic understanding of trading and the marketplace. There are many resources both offline and on — books, articles, reports and publications that will teach you trading basics.

Among the smartest things you can do is study the daily habits of winning traders. You will most likely find that they trade with a plan, analyze every trade and keep accurate records. Most traders know how much to trade, accept that not all trades will be winners and rarely if ever make the same mistake twice.

Capital – Aside from the obvious, "how much money are you prepared to risk," most trading systems have recommended equity requirements. Whether it's starting with $5,000 or as much as $100,000,000 you need to decide what portion of your overall investment portfolio can be allocated toward futures trading. Savings for college, retirement or emergencies should not be included in that number.

Risk Tolerance – Probably the most important aspect of any trading endeavor, whether using a trading system or not, is the ability to withstand losses and continue with your plan. Every individual is unique and has different risk tolerance levels. So, before you enter into a trade, determine how much of a loss you're willing to accept.

Whether you express it as a dollar figure or percent of the margin amount, you should always keep some money in reserve. Nobody wins all the time in trading. Setting limits upfront will lessen the risk of emotional decisions should the market turn against you.

Single Market versus Multi-Commodity Systems — Single market systems are designed with a unique trading methodology targeted for exposure to specific markets of interest. Trading focus ranges from the S&P 500 to Bonds, Currencies or Metals.

On the other hand, multi-commodity systems provide trade instructions for more than one market sector and, of course, offer a broader spectrum of market exposure. Many Multi-commodity systems are designed for trade across all market sectors.

Time & Patience-There is the time you spend in day to day trading activities – and the timeframe of trades in your system. Both are considerations in the system(s) you end up choosing. The duration of the trades that a system generates can range from quick trades for small, short-term profits to long-term trades aimed at capturing trends over a period of month. Since trading futures is a long term proposition and losses will be inevitably sustained over time, patience is paramount to your success.

Choosing A Broker – While you don't have to be a market analyst or trading guru to succeed, the vast majority of system developers recommend that investors employ the services of a reputable system execution broker. Since many systems require constant monitoring, using a broker can eliminate virtually all the work associated with a system.

Wisdom Financial specializes in providing commodity futures managed account services. We will be happy to explain how the system you select can be traded for you. If you are a new investor, we can also assist you in constructing a diversified portfolio by allocating risk capital to professional commodity trading advisors and proven commodity trading systems.

6 Golden Rules For Effective System Trading

While there is no textbook approach to selecting a trading system, your ultimate success hinges largely on your ability to develop good trading habits. While phrases like "the trend is your friend," or "cut your losses and let your profits ride" are accurate, you need to understand the substance behind them.

Rule #1: Make sure you're properly capitalized. Your account must be able to sustain a draw down under the program without incurring a margin call that forces you out of the system before upside performance begins.

Rule #2: Have a plan and stick to it. Enter, exit and place your protective stops as the system dictates. Don't hold back on taking a trading signal with the hope of getting a better price. As mentioned earlier, it is only by adhering to a preconceived formula that you can resist the temptations and emotional stresses that are inherent to a speculative situation.

Rule #3: Set definite risk parameters. By setting limits from the get go, you'll lessen the risk of emotional decision making. The truth is that people who are not in a position to accept losses (either psychologically or financially) should not be trading.

Rule #4: Diversify. Rather than exposing your entire trading account to a position in one futures contract, trade with markets, systems and timeframes that are unique in their methodology. This diversification is aimed at reducing the overall risk and exposure in any individual system or portfolio.

Rule #5: Study past performance. Most system developers maintain websites where you can view performance statistics. While some actually do show results based on actual trading, most provide hypothetical results accumulated by back-testing their strategies on past market data.

Since hypothetical results are prepared with the benefit of hindsight, they do not reflect true financial risk. However, you can still view past performance as a good starting point for research. You can evaluate key performance statistics such as current year-to-date return, average return, average winning trade, maximum draw down, average draw down and average losing trade.

Rule #6: Consult with an unbiased source. One of the best ways to learn more about the actual performance of trading systems is to seek out advice from those actively trading them. At Wisdom Financial our trading team provides valuable and objective guidance on trading systems. Since we receive no compensation for the sale of trading systems we recommend, you will get candid feedback that is in your best interest. Naturally, we have a vested interest in your success and helping you to meet your trading objectives.

What You Can Expect From Wisdom Financials System Management Team

No question about it, futures trading is high risk. And, though the innovations in trading software can help you increase your odds, there are many other factors that go into successful trading. At Wisdom Financial we pride ourselves on providing a level of customer service and cutting edge investment products that is unsurpassed in the industry. We will do whatever it takes to help you meet your goals.

Together, our systems management professionals have over 20 years of combined experience executing mechanical trading systems for individuals, corporations and commodity training advisors. If you want us to 'hold your hand' every step of the way, we will do that. And, if you want more control of the process, that, too, is your choice.

As a client of Wisdom Financial, you will be assigned a personal broker who will play a key role in the day to day activities involved with managing your system(s) of choice. We will provide guidance on choosing a system, and help you put your trading plan into action. The day-to-day work is all handled for you – downloading data, generating trading orders and sending those orders to the exchange floor for execution.

During the trading session you will receive a fax or email detailing each transaction. Plus, you will receive a follow-up fax or email each evening showing you the positions you have, margin required, and profits or losses from the previous trading session. You also will be able to check into your account's real-time activity at a secure web site anytime day or night.

Taking advantage of these services will ensure that all of the rules for successful trading are followed. It also means that you can devote your time to the things you want to do, not what your system tells you to do.

Chapter 4 – This is How CoolTrade Explains It

http://www.cool-trade.com/education/choosesoftware.asp

How to Choose the Best Automated Stock Trading Software
By Regina Guinn

Get the information you need to evaluate stock trading software

In today's market, investors are wondering if they should even buy stocks and if they can make money. The answer to both is "yes." Stock market trading is a wonderful opportunity now, with prices lower and volatility higher than in many years. Stock trading online has never been more popular.

Automated trading platforms, robotic trading programs, online day trading systems--there are many terms used to describe the stock trading systems that can help you to make a stock investment and to grow your money. Review the criteria below and understand your own personal preferences by talking with other stock traders. Identify the facts you need to compare programs.

You'll need a good understanding of the automated trading tools' features and costs before you make a decision.

Many types of companies offer stock trading advice and stock trading strategies. They run the gamut from educational programs that aim to teach you how to trade, to a list of recommended stocks to buy and sell at certain triggers, to brokerage firm proprietary software. With such a variety, how do you choose? This article will guide you through the features and benefits of the programs that are available for online stock trading. We will not discuss trading software for options or Forex trading. Many of the programs are geared towards "day traders," who technically open long positions (buy) or short positions (sell short) and close these positions the same day. Not everyone who uses these programs closes out their positions by the end of the trading day--sometimes they hold their positions for days, weeks or months. We'll call this "active trading." Sometimes this is also referred to as "swing trading."

The essential features of a stock trading program include a data feed for stock quotes and indicators, stock charts or charting capability of major indicators, current balance and positions and an order entry system. The order entry system should allow stop (loss) orders, stop limit orders and trailing stops. A trailing stop limit is similar to the stop (loss), except its loss will be measured from the stocks highest point achieved. The preferred method would be to keep the trigger prices in stealth mode, not viewable by the market makers, rather than as actual orders. Most automated trading software should include a watch list of the stocks to potentially trade based on the parameters the stock trader has entered.

Exchange Traded Funds (ETF's) can be part of an efficient trading strategy. These are mutual funds that are traded intraday on the stock exchanges, unlike traditional mutual funds that are a basket of securities priced at the close of the market. Online stock trading systems should also include trading capabilities for ETFs.

Other features to look for include safety measures that stock traders may take, such as establishing a profit goal--the minimum price increase a trader would expect a stock to gain before closing their position. Also highly desirable is a form of profit protection for your investments, which is the reduced profit goal. After the stock reaches its profit goal and continues to rise, the stock trading software should wait and let the profit increase. If the stock price decreases or pulls back, the online trading program should close the position and lock the profit. This pullback value should not have any effect before the profit goal is reached and is intended to improve stock performance. More sophisticated auto trading programs will also offer the percentage gain from stock trader's entry price, and the trader can also specify a minimum amount in case the percentage gained is too low.

Check the features and ask questions

Number of Technical Indicators - There are literally hundreds of indicators that stock traders can use to determine which stocks to buy and sell and when. The most robust programs will offer hundreds of indicators for technical analysis, such as Bollinger Bands, and some will even include indicators for Candlestick Chart formations. Robotic programs use these indicators to set conditions under which online investing will occur.

Complexity - Automated stock trading programs vary greatly in ease of use. Some online stock trading systems do require actual programming expertise. Others are simply point and click. Check out the online demo to see that it fits your level of comfort before making a commitment. Talk to others who are currently using the auto trading websites and check out their online communities for more comments.

Number of Long and Short Strategies Per Account - Due to the size of the online trading platform, there may be a limit to the number of strategies that you can have loaded on each account. If you want to run, say two long trading strategies, then you may need two accounts. Also confirm if you have enough memory on your computer for two or more accounts. Experienced active traders may run two or more live long and short strategies, while having additional accounts for strategies that they are testing in a simulator mode

Find out how advanced your software can be

Recommended Additional Features - The best automated stock trading software will include additional features that active traders will find invaluable once they have begun automated trading.

Additional strategy and order entry features include the ability to add to a position as a stock goes up, or as the stock declines, as well as a minimum purchase interval that the stock price should drop before it begins purchasing additional shares. A maximum bid/ask range will also be helpful, as the size of the spread can directly impact a swing trader's ability to make profitable trades.

If there are hundreds of indicators, as is the case with robotic traders, see if the definitions of the indicators are readily available. The definition or formula for indicators may vary from one electronic trading platform to another, so be sure you understand them first.

Recommend you have a program that displays current Profit and Loss (P&L) on your open positions and the status of the rules on your watch list. For example, if a stock on the watch list hasn't traded, is there a feature where the trader can pull up the rules and indicators to see which one(s) is preventing the trade?

Some automated stock trading programs visually display the percentage of symbols up and down in each sector from the specified time frame to the current time so you can see how the market is turning. Does the platform include the ability to block certain symbols from trading? If you're running a long trading strategy, you won't want to be buying ETF's that short the market.

Day traders will want automated trading software that tracks and displays the number of day trades remaining. Day trading is regulated by the SEC, so it's important to understand if you will be day trading first.

Orders in Stealth Mode - A standard feature of many trading software programs is the ability to enter limit, stop and stop limit orders. While it is important to have an exit strategy from your positions, telegraphing it to the institutional traders in the form of publicly viewed limits is not. It's a little like poker--whoever can see all the hands has the advantage. Instead, newer programs allow the user to enter these price points in the auto trader system, but trigger a market order when the conditions are met. This is one advantage of a truly robotic stock trading program.

Automatically Executes Your Trading Strategy Even While You're Away From Your Computer - Very few stock market trading systems can actually do this. For those that do, it's done based on the trader selecting technical indicators, comparison operators and numerical inputs that will activate opening, adding to, or closing stock positions. Essentially, it's a rules driven software system. The trader can select from hundreds of historical indicators representing the stocks' previous conditions. The indicators should be updated daily using the latest data. Programs that can trade automatically are the cream of the online investing software crop. They take the emotion out of investing. Long time traders report that the simplest strategies, when left to run on their own for long periods perform best. The program should also have a manual override so the stock trader can manually place a trade as well. Specifically ask if the system has this capability. Many market themselves as "automated trading" but are not truly automated.

Ability to Simulate Strategies In Real Time Before Running Live - Most traders would agree that they'd like to "test drive" a system before using it. Some programs allow this through "back-testing," in which the program uses past data to execute the trades and show you what they would have been. This is not always accurate, as there is much data needed to perform a thorough back-test and it's nearly impossible to replicate all the circumstances with just the historical data. In addition, how the system performed in a market last month or last year does not indicate how it will perform in the here and now. There are a few systems that allow the stock trader to simulate strategies, but this is done mostly with paper tickets, rather than through the software package. The best stock trading software will let you practice stock trading using a live real-time data feed during market hours. This is the preferred method, as it gives traders a very realistic view of how their trading strategy is performing and the ability to feel the highs and lows of daily trading without investing real money. If you can simulate trades, you won't need to open an actual brokerage account until you go "live" with real money. Ask if there is a limit on how long you can run in the simulation mode.

Shows You How to Create A Stock Trading Strategy - There should be a step by step walk through to show novice traders how to create a trading strategy. Are there off-the-shelf strategies that are available for your use? Are there any fees involved or are they offered for free? Can you modify the off the shelf strategies? Note that firms should not be guaranteeing you a certain return. The best firms will have long and short stock trading strategies available at no charge and will allow the stock trader to create their own. Some firms will even allow you to copy strategies from a "friends" list. One size does not fit all. If the company doesn't tell you the details of the strategy or why they selected or recommend a certain stock, then it's not advisable to use it. You may overpay for "proprietary" services and may be able to obtain free stock market tips and recommendations online that will perform comparably.

Tech Support and Customer Service - The best automated stock trading software firms have an extremely high "up-time" and are very rarely out of service. Check on the firm's record--how often have they had outages? The software should be easy to install and should work with a variety of operating systems (Windows XP, Windows Vista, etc.). If you have questions, is there a knowledgeable and helpful staff to provide service? How quickly do they respond, if by email?

Commissions - Trading commissions can eat into your profits if you are not careful about choosing a plan that fits your needs. Commissions can vary greatly from broker to broker, depending on the number of shares traded, whether the shares are in round lots of 100, price of the shares traded and the number of trades you place each month. Stock traders may even want to have more than one account if they have a trading strategy that normally trades 100 shares lots and another that trades 1000 share lots. It pays to read the fine print.

Number of Broker Choices - If you have a proprietary brokerage software product, then you'll only be able to trade through that firm. The best online trading includes the lowest commissions for the typical trades for each strategy that you use. There are other programs whose software has been integrated into the order placing functionality at a variety of brokerage firms. Commissions will be one consideration in choosing a firm. Another is the margin rates. If you choose to have a margin account and borrow against the value of your securities to open more positions, you will be charged margin interest. Rates will vary by firm.

Typically, firms with the lowest commissions won't pay you interest or offer a money market fund for your uninvested cash. This is how they keep their costs down. If you anticipate having extra cash that you won't use for trading, you may want to keep it in another account where it can earn more. You should also check if there is a minimum to open an account or a minimum number of trades required.

Check the costs and software support

Initial Software Fee and Monthly Fees - Ask is there is an initial fee to buy the software package. Is it thousands of dollars? If so, find out what you are really getting. Much of what you can obtain from some of these programs can be found in inexpensive books or on the Internet for free. Is there also a monthly fee? If so, what does it cover? In reviewing online trading services, more expensive software is not necessarily better. Some active investing services are less expensive because they have more subscribers.

Data Feed Fee - Does the program include real time data feeds for stock quotes and indicators? Is there an extra fee for this or is it included in the basic monthly fee? This is the biggest component cost in developing automated stock trading programs. Or, is the data delayed by 20 minutes? Is it only the end of day data? If so, even in a simulation, old data is not good data. Many brokerage firms offer free Level II quotes to qualified active traders who trade a specified number of trades each month.

Stock Charts Fee - How will you review the major indicators that you're using to make trading decisions? Some programs include stock charts with their fee; others charge a separate fee for it. Depending on the platform you choose, you may or may not need a charting package. Find out how much is it and how much you can customize the stock charts to track your favorite indicators.

Ongoing Support Fee - Ask is there are any other fees. Hidden fees will definitely each into a stock trader's profits. If you're not in the market to make money, then you shouldn't be in the market.

Long Term Contract - Is the fee you're paying upfront for a year's contract? If so, is it automatically renewed every year?

Training Fee - Find out if there is a separate training fee. For programs that market themselves as financial educators, there will be a fee, sometimes hundreds or thousands of dollars, as this is how they make their money. The best automated stock trading software programs provide free training.

Training Formats - Is the training in the form of a live seminar? Webinar? Are there extra materials such as DVDs that you must buy to find out all the information advertised? Or, is live training available in the company's office?

Minimum to Invest - Brokerage firms have their own

minimums but there are also account minimum balances required by the Securities and Exchange Commission (SEC) for what it calls "pattern day traders." A day trade occurs when a trader opens and closes the same position in a margin account on the same day. A pattern day trader is any person who executes 4 or more day trades within 5 business days in a margin account, provided the number of day trades is more than 6% of the total trades in the account during that period. All pattern day traders must maintain a minimum of $25,000 in equity at all times.

System Requirements - The more robust the trading system, the greater the memory requirements. Check this before you sign up or purchase a new computer. If you sign up for more than one account, will your machine have enough RAM to run both or will you need to purchase an extra computer or more memory? If you have a Mac, ask if the software works on Mac, as not all do. You may want to have one computer dedicated only to your automated stock trading programs and not run other word processing or spreadsheet programs.

Trading Strategy Statistics - In addition to Reports, another great feature is strategy statistics. They will tell the serious stock trader the number of trades executed and break them down by profitable vs. unprofitable over various intervals. Reviewing the strategy accuracy increases the odds that a stock trader will be profitable.

Online Trading Community - Trading platform developers who are truly proud of their work welcome comments and questions from users. Take some time to read their stock trading forum and see what other stock traders are saying. There are even a few automated stock trading programs that will take requests for additional indicators from their users.

Take the right steps as you choose stock trading software

Be wary of those who tell you that you must follow their stock trading system using only their tools. This is about you having control over your financial future. There as many successful stock trading strategies as there are active traders. Experiment, talk to others and do research. You will find what works best for you.

Use caution when signing up for anything long-term, even if a 30-day free trial is offered. Some firms may request a large down payment or full payment in advance and pressure you on the spot, promising a discount if you sign up immediately. Some consumers have reported difficulty in obtaining refunds even when they have followed the procedures exactly.

Happy trading!

Chapter 5 – This is How Binary Options Explains It

http://nischalmaniar.info/choosing-the-best-trading-platform/

Binary Options – Best Brokers, Best Strategies, Recent News » Articles » Choosing the Best Trading Platform

Choosing the Best Trading Platform

Forex trading is becoming increasingly popular, but what many Forex traders aren't aware of is the technique of trading currencies through binary options; a much easier and less complex method for trading currencies. Binary options also have the benefit of a very low barrier to entry. Perhaps most enticing for many traders is the fact that you can make returns on your investments ranging from 60 to 500 percent!

There are many brokers online who offer trading in binary options with very competitive payouts. In addition to trading currencies, binary options also allow you to trade in stocks, commodities, and indices all on the same account. Charting packages offered from many of the brokers will give you all the data and tools necessary to get started with all of these financial instruments.

Binary Options Trading Systems

When trading with many of the online brokers you will find payouts that range from 60 to 70 percent. While that may seem on the low side, these brokers also offer up to 15% payback on any losses. This has the benefit of limiting the amount you can lose on any one trade, while still offering attractive payouts when your trades go in the right direction. Even so, many people hesitate at the prospect of receiving a 70% payout on a win versus an 85% loss. The way to get around this discrepancy is to use a solid binary options trading system.

Trading systems let you use history as your guide to predicting the future movements of financials. The best systems increase your odds of winning trades, and thereby increase your overall profits.

Even though research shows that roughly 80% of all options expire worthless, the use of a profitable system can simplify your trading and ensure that your wins outnumber your losses. Best of all, once a system is proven to generate winning trades, you can automate it to trade effortlessly. Every trader should strive to find a system that they can trade automatically, thus taking any guesswork or emotion out of their trading.

Binary Options Platforms

Different brokers will offer different platforms for trading binary options. Most are easy to learn to use and their powerful charting and analysis features will help take your trading to the next level. You should take the time to explore several trading platforms to determine which of them will best suit your needs. As with almost everything, the platform that is right for your neighbor may not be the same one that is right for you. Just as some people like Apple computers and some like Windows computers.

Here is a quick overview of some different binary options platforms available to you:

Web based and standalone platforms: These platforms are quite powerful and can help your trading success. You do need to be aware of the hidden costs inherent in some of these systems however. User friendliness, speed of execution, maintenance and data sources should all be considered when evaluating the web and standalone platforms.

Multi-instrument trading platform: The binary options brokers allow you to trade a wide variety of financial instruments, but only if the platform you are using supports this. If you plan on diversifying into multiple financial markets or currencies you need to be sure the platform has support for this type of trading.

Secure Trading Platform: Always ensure that the platform you are using has sufficient encryption levels to protect your data and trades. 128 bit SSL encryption is pretty standard these days, but if you can get better security you can trade more at ease.

Out Of the Money Platform: When you are trading binary options, every single penny can make a difference. This is why we recommend that you find a broker and platform that supports payback for out of the money options. This will help limit your risk on each trade and will theoretically increase your profits.

Minimum Deposit Platform

Many binary options platforms have minimum deposits of several hundred dollars. Some brokers understand that this is excessive for beginning traders and they have begun offering trading on platforms for as little as $30. If you have limited starting capital you will want to find one of these minimum deposit platforms for binary option trading.

Chapter 6 – This is How Randolph Read Explains It

http://www.randolphread.com/affordable-online-trading-system

10 Things to Consider (Other Than Price) When Choosing an Affordable Trading Online System

If you are going to make your own trading decisions in a self-directed account, you have the option of trading by phone with a live broker or online through a trading system. In choosing a trading online system, affordability is an important factor. But if you are an active trader or a professional trade manager, you also should look for a system that accommodates your trading style rather than requiring you to change to fit its parameters. If you settle for yesterday's technology or for systems or order routing that don't meet your needs, you could end up dissatisfied and shopping around again.

1. Market

Does this online trading system make available true direct market access to the major global futures exchanges on which I want to trade?

2. Pit trading

Does it also offer an efficient and responsive procedure for trading pit contracts?

3. Strategy support

Does the online system allow me to effectively apply complex trading strategies (OCO, GTC, FOK, IOC STP LIMIT, Trading Stops, Brackets, etc.)?

4. Up-to-date information

Will I need a separate subscription to an external data vendor to access streaming quotes, price alerts or news feed customized to my preferred contracts?

5. Technical charting

Are the built-in charting function, chart styles, and indicators I wish to employ available?

6. Advanced customization

Does it allow me to customize indicators?

7. Detailed reports

Will I need additional software in order to generate detailed, custom reports?

8. Institutional trading

Can it meet my special needs as a CTA or professional trade manager? For the creation of allocation block accounts without back office trade reconciliation? For the efficient handling of large batches of trades?

9. Storage and reliability

If I temporarily lose connectivity between my computer and the server, will my working orders still process?

10. Tech support

Is sufficient tech support available online or phone in order to keep me up and operating when I need to be?

These questions are designed to get you started. Not all "affordable" online trading systems are going to meet your needs. Based on your own specific trading requirements, you will probably have additional queries. An efficient, affordable online system can help you boost your bottom line, so find one that will work well for you.

If you are interested in a broker-assisted, full service account, call 1-866-840-9075 or email us at support@randolphread.com to set up a personal phone consultation.

Our experienced brokers and advisors help investors understand, navigate, interpret and trade the commodities futures and futures options markets. With a thorough understanding of the importance of managing risk, and the unique characteristics of traded commodity, index, financial, and currency contracts, we develop customized advice based on each client's unique set of needs, motivations, understanding and expectations.

Chapter 7 – This is How InvestorGuide.com Explains It

Choosing an Online Forex Trading Platform

http://www.investorguide.com/igu-article-1152-forex-trading-choosing-an-online-forex-trading-platform.html

InvestorGuide University > Subject: Forex > Topic: Forex Trading > Choosing an Online Forex Trading Platform by Tony Siragusa

With today's volatile economic climate and a consistently weak American dollar, the concept of speculating in foreign currency exchange is becoming increasingly attractive.

Yet many investors still are not very familiar with the practice, and taking time to learn the tricks of the trade is easier said than done. That's where online trading tools come in: learning about and participating in foreign currency exchange online provides access to the markets which were only previously accessible to institutional users.

As with any form of speculation, the smartest and most financially responsible approach is to know what opportunities are available, and what different online Forex platforms have to offer before jumping in.

Perhaps the most important factor of online currency exchange – especially for novices – is a user-friendly experience, a factor from which everything else trickles down. By nature, foreign exchange markets are not the easiest to master, but finding the right online platform will allow for greater ease in transitions for newcomers.

Currency trading platform Easy-Forex™ (http://www.easy-forex.com/us), for example, is set up so that a customer of any skill set could reasonably begin trading within a few minutes of logging onto the site. With reliable internet access, you're well on your way.

Unlike many online trading platforms, there's no need for software downloads of any kind with Easy-Forex. Its web-based program makes no impact on your computer hardware and provides speed to trading for account users.

Not always the case in online trading platforms, new traders can begin trading immediately with Easy-Forex, with a minimum deposit of $200. Easy-Forex was at the forefront in the industry to accept credit card deposits in addition to more traditional payment options.

Obviously, one of online trading's biggest advantages is the ability to eliminate the broker as a middle man. However, traders still often require real-time assistance, and the best online currency exchange platforms insist on establishing relationships with each trader. Easy-Forex offers support from Account Service Managers at all hours when the Forex market is open—24 hours a day, 5½ days a week—via phone, email or advanced online chat.

Easy-Forex utilizes tools like guided video tours, training materials (http://en.easy-forex.com/US/eBook.aspx) and one-on-one training to ensure that investors are well-equipped to trade Forex online, regardless of their experience level. You can visit its dedicated web training tools here.

Though brokers conventionally carry business hours, foreign currency exchange markets allow trading 24 hours a day over 5½ days a week. Since the internet never shuts down, traders using an online platform gain greater accessibility and flexibility.

As with all web sites that utilize credit cards and other private information, security should be a primary concern for every online trading application. Make sure that whatever platform you choose offers highly encrypted security measures.

Many over-the-counter online platforms are quite similar in terms of their offers and opportunities, but

Easy-Forex remains an innovator in the field, with several unique tools available to every trader:

- The *Inside Viewer*™ is a proprietary tool that allows transparency so you know what others on the Easy-Forex platform are trading in real-time. View the popularity and direction of the buy or sell of a specific currency pair as well as their average entry, stop loss and take profit rates.
- The *Trade Controller*™ allows you to visually adjust the parameters of your open deals and check out alternative scenarios. This feature's stop loss element is notable, which allows you to set your own risk parameters.
- The freeze rate capability, a unique feature where Easy-Forex allows you to hold an exchange rate constant for several seconds. Regardless of rate movements, the freeze guarantees your rate for that period of time with no commitment to trade.

As you can see, there's a lot to consider with online foreign currency exchange. By making the right choices, you gain control over the level of convenience and security you experience in your trading ventures.

Chapter 8 – This is How The Minimalist Guide Explains It

The Minimalist Guide To Choosing The Best Forex Trading System

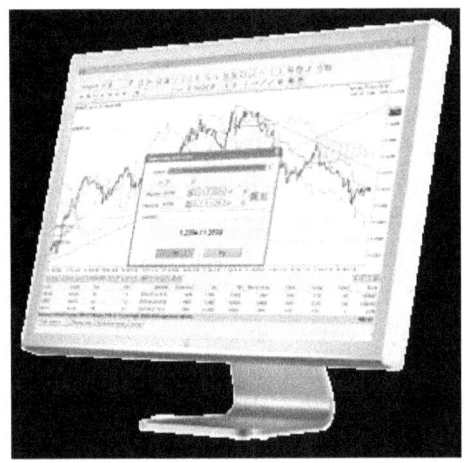

http://getforextradingstrategies.com/the-minimalist-guide-to-choosing-the-best-forex-trading-system/

If you are new to the Forex market or if you have been trading currencies for a while, you will agree with me that sometimes, trading can be a little bit sophisticated and for you to understand the market more and for you to trade more carefully, you will need a Forex trading system that will help to reduce the work that you have to be trading currencies. These different Forex trading systems help to bring the trading languages to the level that you will understand and with that, you will make better trading decisions.

If you are looking for the best trading system that you will use in trading activities, you will come across many trading systems that will promise you the very best in Forex trading, these different systems will assure you the best ways to make profits, the easiest ways for you to monitor the market and know when to trade. These systems will sometimes be too good in the ads that you might even want fall for their different wimps but you need to be careful so that you don't end up getting the wrong system that only promises but does not fulfill.

The minimalist guide on how to choose the best Forex trading system will guide you on how you can in the midst of hundreds of thousands of trading systems that you will see in your search for trading system that you can use in your trading activities, make the right choice on the system that you can use that will get the very best of results in your trading activities. In the next paragraphs are different tips that will guide you through your choice of Forex trading systems.

Purpose of The System

The first thing that will guide you on choosing the best Forex trading system that will be very useful is you knowing the purpose you want the trading system to achieve for you. Going in search of a trading system without having a clear cut objective that you want it to achieve for you can make you end up choosing the right trading system for the wrong purpose

Having traded in the Forex market for almost five years, I can tell you this from experience, from my own experience and from those that I have seen trading in the market. This is not a mistake that you would like to make when you can rid yourself of the disappointments, waste of time and money. So, for you to avoid such mistake, take out time to determine the purpose that you want the Forex trading system to achieve for you, before you go on your search for trading system.

Cost of The System

Most people make the mistake of getting a trading system that is not expensive or the one that won't cost them much. For you to get the best trading system, you have to spend some money to get it. This is because the results that a cheap trading will give can never be compared to the results that a trading system this expensive will give you. For example, most of us have cars in our homes; can a car that is worth $5,000 give the same result with a car that is worth $25,000? Of course it will not, they are two cars on totally different levels. The same way with trading systems. A trading system that is less expensive will not give standard results that you need to trade exceptionally well in the Forex market.

History of The System

Everything that has ever existed in this world has a history whether it is a good thing or a bad thing. So if anyone tells you that there is nothing like a trading system history, don't believe it. You have to find the history of the system that you are planning to get for your various activities in the Forex market.

In getting any system, you have to make sure that it has a very good history that other traders like you can attest to, if not, don't bother getting the system. Any system that has ever been created or designed for trading in the Forex market has a history and you have to find out the history of any trading system you are planning to get.

The different things that you need to know about the system's history include; when it was created or designed, the kind of response that it had when it was introduced into the market, if it was accepted, the different reasons why people accepted it and if it wasn't accepted, the reasons why traders didn't accept it and so on. You can think of other things that you can find out about the history of the trading system.

The Nature of the System

Talking about the nature of the system, I mean if the system is something that easy to understand and use? When choosing a Forex trading system, you should try as much as possible to go for trading systems that are easy to use. If you are going to achieve a great success with a trading system, then you have to make sure that you get trading system that will be very easy for you to understand. The system should be able to interpret the various trading signals that it is giving to you so that you will know what decision you can make regarding the trading of currencies.

The more simple a trading system is, the more you will be able to detect and read meaning into the different signals that it shows you and with that you can make good decisions in the Forex market.

There many trading systems that you can find in the Forex market if you are looking a trading system, but you have to be careful in your choice of a Forex trading system, because your overall success in the Forex market will be determined by how well you make trading decisions and with a good Forex trading system, you can be sure that you will make better decisions.

I Have a Special Gift for My Readers

I appreciate my readers for without them I am just another struggling author attempting to make ends meet.

My readers and I have in common a passion for the written word as well as the desire to learn and grow from books.

My special offer to you is a massive ebook library that I have compiled over the years. It contains hundreds of fiction and non-fiction ebooks in Adobe Acrobat PDF format as well as the Greek classics and old literary classics too.

In fact, this library is so massive to completely download the entire library will require over 5 GBs open on your desktop.

Use the link below and scan all of the ebooks in the library. You can select the ebooks you want individually or download the entire library.

The link below does not expire after a given time period so you are free to return for more books rather than clog your desktop. And feel free to give the link to your friends who enjoy reading too.

I thank you for reading my book and hope if you are pleased that you will leave me an honest review so that I can improve my work and or write books that appeal to your interests.

Okay, here is the link...

http://tinyurl.com/special-readers-promo

PS: If you wish to reach me personally for any reason you may simply write to mailto:support@epubwealth.com.

I answer all of my emails so rest assured I will respond.

Meet the Author

Meet the Author
Dr. Leland Benton is Director of Applied Web Info, a holding company for ePubWealth.com, a leading ePublisher company based in Utah. With over 21,000 resellers in over 22-countries, ePubWealth.com is a leader in ePublishing, book promotion, and ebook marketing.

As the creator and author of "The ePubWealth Program," Leland teaches up-and-coming authors the ins-and-outs of today's ePublishing world. He has assisted hundreds of authors make it big in the ePublishing world.

Leland also created a series of external book promotion programs and teaches authors how to promote their books using external marketing sources.

Leland is also the Managing Director of Applied Mind Sciences, the company's mind research unit and Chief Forensics Investigator for the company's ForensicsNation unit. He is active in privacy rights through the company's PrivacyNations unit and is an expert in survival planning and disaster relief through the company's SurvivalNations unit.

Leland resides in Southern Utah.

Visit some of his websites
http://appliedmindsciences.com/
http://appliedwebinfo.com/
http://BoolbuilderPLUS.com
http://embarrassingproblemsfix.com/
http://www.epubwealth.com/
http://forensicsnation.com/
http://neternatives.com/
http://privacynations.com/
http://survivalnations.com/
http://thebentonkitchen.com
http://theolegions.org

www.ingramcontent.com/pod-product-compliance
Lightning Source LLC
Chambersburg PA
CBHW071812170526
45167CB00003B/1285